# PREDATORS

Jillian Powell

Editorial consultants: Cliff Moon,
Lorraine Petersen and Frances Ridley

RISING★STARS

**nasen**

NASEN House, 4/5 Amber Business Village, Amber Close, Amington, Tamworth, Staffordshire B77 4RP

**Rising Stars UK Ltd.**
22 Grafton Street, London W1S 4EX
www.risingstars-uk.com

Published 2007
Reprinted 2009

Cover design: Button plc
Cover image: Alamy
Text design and typesetting: Andy Wilson
Publisher: Gill Budgell
Project management and editorial: Lesley Densham
Editing: Clare Robertson
Editorial consultants: Cliff Moon, Lorraine Petersen and Frances Ridley
Technical adviser: Mandy Holloway (NHM)
Illustrations: Chris King: pages 14–15, 24–25, 36–39
Photos: Alamy: pages 4–5, 6, 7, 8, 9, 11, 13, 16, 17, 18–19, 20, 22, 23, 26, 27, 28, 30, 31, 32–33, 34, 35, 40, 41, 43
Corbis: pages 6, 10, 12, 21, 23, 29, 42
Kobal: page 33

British Library Cataloguing in Publication Data.
A CIP record for this book is available from the British Library.

ISBN: 978-1-84680-188-4

Printed by Craft Print International Limited, Singapore

# Contents

# Hunter and prey

**Predators** are animals that eat other animals.

There are predators in the air, on land and in the sea.

Some are skilled hunters. Others lie in wait and **ambush** their **prey**.

If they don't eat, they die. It's life or death in the wild.

# Killing machines

Predators are designed to kill.

### Sharp eyes

These help predators spot their prey before it spots them.

Eagle eyes see four times further than human eyes.

### Powerful jaws

These help predators grip on to their prey and not let go.

A spotted hyena has the strongest jaws of any meat-eater. It can even bite through bone.

### Pointed teeth

Sharp, pointed teeth can slice into hides and meat.

## Strong legs

Predators that hunt are built for speed.

A cheetah can go from 0 to 50 mph in three seconds!

## Sharp claws and talons

Knife-sharp claws and **talons** grab and hold on to prey.

## Secret weapons

Some predators have secret weapons. They use chemicals, poisons or **sonic** booms to stun their prey!

# Big cats

Big cats are big game hunters. They **stalk**, chase and jump to kill their **prey**.

powerful body

keen eyesight: six times better than a human's in the dark

camouflage coat

sharp, pointed teeth

# Tigers

Tigers are the largest cats.

Tigers can grow up to four metres long, and weigh up to 350 kilograms. They can bring down deer and bison.

# Lions

Most big cats hunt alone, but lions hunt in groups and share their kill.

Only one in six chases ends in a kill. So lions aim for big prey like wildebeest and zebras.

# Cheetahs

Cheetahs are the fastest animals on land.
They can run at speeds of up to 70 mph.

A cheetah grabs **prey** with its claws.
It knocks the prey down and kills it
by biting its neck.

At full speed, a cheetah covers
seven metres with a stride.

All four feet are off the ground
for up to half the time!

# Jaguars

Jaguars have powerful jaws. They kill prey with one bite.

They can climb trees to catch monkeys.

They can even drag fish out of water.

# Leopards

Leopards sometimes drag their kill up into a tree. This keeps it away from other **predators**.

**Leopard facts!**

Snow leopards can leap up to ten times their body length. They can strike prey three times their own size.

# Bears

## Polar bears

Polar bears are the biggest land **predators**. They are incredible hunters. They feed on seabirds, whales, seals and walruses.

Polar bears can smell **prey** from over 60 kilometres away.

They break the ice and pull prey out with their powerful claws.

### Polar bear facts!

Height: up to 2.6 metres tall when standing.

Weight: up to 410 kilograms.

They can eat 45 kilograms of seal blubber in one meal.

# Brown bears

Brown bears start a hunt by sniffing the air.

They circle their prey, then jump. They can knock down elk, caribou and moose.

They are also skilled fishers.
They grab fish with their teeth or claws.

**Brown bear facts!**

A brown bear can stand two metres tall and weigh up to 300 kilograms.

# A Snake @ School
## (Part one)

It was 'Bring a Pet to School' day, and the school was raising money for charity.

Students would give short talks about their pets. The most popular pet would win a prize.

George and Darren read the rules.

"It just says all dogs on leads," Darren said. "And cage animals must be kept in their cages."

"That's okay, then," George said. "I can bring Henry!"

"Are you mad?" Darren said. "You can't bring a snake! You'll freak everyone out!"

"Exactly!" George said. "I can't wait to see the look on that Carla's face! Serves her right for turning down a date. And I want Henry to meet Todd Baxter. I'll show Todd for taking my place in the football team!"

Continued on page 24

# Pack hunters

Hyenas, wolves and wild dogs hunt in **packs**.

## Hyenas

Hyenas hunt mainly by night.
They whoop when they get
together to hunt.

They track their **prey** by sight,
hearing and smell.

Hyenas eat every bit of an animal,
even its teeth and bones.

# Wolves

Wolves eat the best parts of a kill first. They hide the rest in snow or ice.

This keeps it fresh for later.

# Snakes

Some snakes kill their **prey** with poison.
They bite their prey with **fangs**.
The fangs inject poison called **venom**.

Other snakes twist round prey and crush it.

### Snake fact!

Snakes can hunt in the dark. They use **pits** in their heads to sense heat from prey.

All snakes swallow their prey whole, by stretching their jaws, skin and stomach.

They can take hours to swallow a meal.

Pythons and boas eat animals as big as goats and deer.

**Snake fact!**

The king cobra's venom is so deadly, one bite could kill an elephant.

# Crocodiles

Crocodiles lie in wait. Then they leap out of the water and grab their **prey**.

They are strong enough to pull a zebra into the water. They roll their prey over to drown it.

Sometimes, groups of crocodiles share a kill.

Crocodiles can grow up to six metres long.

They have over 60 large, cone-shaped teeth.

They have bone-crushing jaws
with a force of over
1325 kilograms per
square centimetre.

**Crocodile fact!**

Beware: on land,
a crocodile can sprint
at up to ten mph —
as fast as a human!

# Spiders

Spiders **ambush** or hunt for their victims.

Some inject their **prey** with **venom**.
Other spiders trap their prey in webs.

Tarantulas ambush their prey.
They rear up and bite it with their
**fangs**. They inject venom and chemicals
which turn prey into liquid they can
suck like soup! Some tarantulas eat
birds, mice, frogs and lizards.

Spiders use many types of web.

orb web

funnel web

## Spider fact!

Spider silk is stronger than Kevlar – a material used for bulletproof vests.

Some webs are over two metres across. They are strong enough to catch birds or bats.

# A Snake @ School
## (Part two)

The classroom was buzzing. People had brought hamsters and rabbits. Carla's dog Benjy was there, with a bow on his head.

George was carrying a large sack.

"What's in the sack?" Todd Baxter asked.

George opened the sack. Henry's head appeared. Then his long body began to slither across the room.

Everyone began screaming. Todd jumped back in shock.

"A … a snake?" he gulped. "I mean … is it poisonous? Why is it putting its tongue out like that?"

"Just seeing what's around!" George grinned. "And no, Henry's not a **venomous** snake."

"Ugh! It's a disgusting slimy snake!" Carla said.

"He's not slimy. He's dry and cold. Look, feel him!" George held Henry up towards Carla. She was not impressed.

Continued on page 36

# Deadly bugs

Scorpions have a deadly sting in their tail.

Scorpions lie in wait under stones. Then they grab their **prey** with powerful **pincers**.

They use their sting to inject **venom**. Then they crush the prey to death.

## Scorpion facts!

Some scorpions grow to 25 centimetres long. They prey on snakes, birds and lizards.

The praying mantis has a stick-like body. It uses **camouflage** to hide.

The mantis grabs its prey with its legs. These have hooks on them that help it grip.

Then the mantis bites off the victim's head!

Giant centipedes grow
up to 25 centimetres long.

Centipedes are fast movers.

On their heads they have claws which inject deadly poison into their prey.

Cone snails are deadly sea snails.

Cone snails **harpoon** fish with venom.

# Ocean predators

The oceans are war zones.

Ocean **predators** use:

- shock attacks
- missiles
- **camouflage**
- chemical weapons
- **sonic** booms.

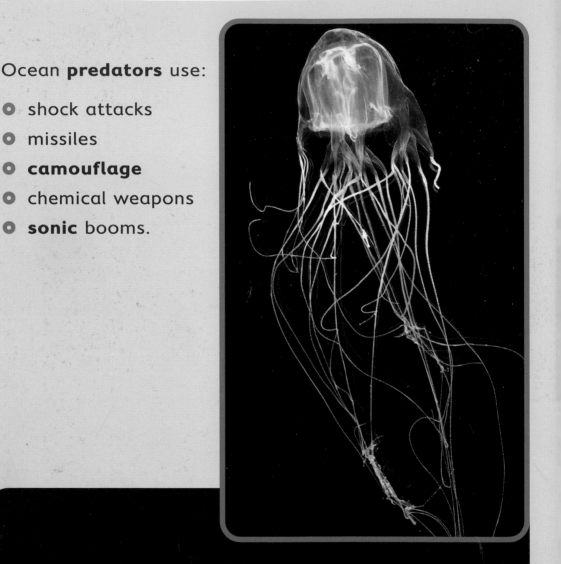

Box jellyfish or 'sea wasps' have 5000 stinging cells on each **tentacle**. The jellyfish use the stinging cells as poison darts to shoot into **prey**.

Dolphins use **sonic** booms to stun their prey. They make bangs and clicking sounds which stun and confuse fish.

**Venomous** lionfish corner their prey using their large fins. They swallow it whole. Lionfish protect themselves from predators with spines that inject **venom**.

# Killer whales

Killer whales hunt like **pack** animals. They circle and herd their **prey**.

They send out **sonic** signals to find prey under water. The signals bounce off prey so the killer whales can 'see' it by sound.

Killer whales swim right up into the surf to catch seals or sea lions.

It takes years for a killer whale to learn this skill.

They can also break through ice to knock prey into the water.

# Great white sharks

Great white sharks are famous **predators**.

**pointed snout**

**sharp eyesight**

**3000 sharp teeth**

Great whites can swim at up to 25 mph. They hunt mainly by sight and smell. They often attack from below.

Great whites eat seabirds, seals, sea lions and fish. They even eat small whales and other sharks. About five attacks a year are on humans.

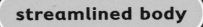
streamlined body

## Shark fact!

The film 'Jaws' (1975) was about a man-eating great white shark.

# Octopuses

Octopuses eat fish, crabs, turtles ... and other octopuses!

They have hundreds of suckers on their **tentacles** to grab victims. If they lose a tentacle, they just grow another!

They can confuse **prey** by squeezing out a cloud of black ink.

The octopus uses its sharp beak to bite and kill its prey. It takes the prey back to its den for a slow meal.

The world's largest octopus is the giant Pacific octopus. It can weigh over 70 kilograms and have an arm span of nine metres.

## Octopus facts!

They have blue blood.

They have three hearts.

They can change shape and colour for **camouflage**.

# A Snake @ School
## (Part three)

Henry was having a good time exploring.

"What does it eat?" someone asked.

"Dead mice," George answered. "We keep them in the freezer."

Everyone said "Yuck!"

"It's getting away!" Carla yelled.

"It's okay. He's gone in the PE cupboard!" George said. "He'll like it in there. Lots of things to climb over."

"Strange sort of pet!" Todd said. "But I heard Jason Briggs in 5D has got a spider."

"Really?" George said. "Is it a tarantula?" He went to see.

It turned out to be a large house spider in a matchbox. But when George came back, Henry had disappeared.

Continued on the next page

It was time for Assembly. Suddenly, everyone started screaming. They all ran for the door.

Henry was slithering across the stage. Then he disappeared through an open window.

George and Darren found him at lunchtime.

"Thank goodness!" Darren said. "No harm done!"

"I'm not sure about that!" George said. "Look at him!" He pointed to Henry's bulging stomach.

"Oh no! What's he eaten?" Darren said. "It could be someone's rabbit. It looks huge!"

Mrs Briggs appeared. She was one of the lunchtime supervisors. "That snake is a hero!" she smiled.

"Hero? He's eaten someone's pet!" Darren said.

"No he hasn't!" Mrs Briggs said. "He's eaten that rat that kept hanging around the bins. And you'd better go inside. He's just won Most Popular Pet!"

# Birds of prey

Birds of **prey** hunt from the air.
They use their powerful eyesight to find prey.

Some birds of prey can spot prey hundreds of metres below. They dive down to grab it with their **talons**.

**Bird of prey fact!**

Falcons can dive at up to 180 mph.

The Andean condor is one of the largest birds of prey. Its wings have a span of three metres. It has a sharp, curved beak and powerful claws. It hunts or **scavenges** for dead prey like cattle, sheep and seals.

# Eagles

Eagles have the best eyesight of all. They can look to the front and sides at the same time.

Eagles can spot a rabbit moving from three kilometres away.

Eagles are powerful flyers.
They can carry off
a sheep or a deer.

The harpy eagle has talons as big
as a brown bear's claws.

They strike with twice the force
of a rifle bullet.

# Quiz

1 Which predator has the strongest jaws?

2 Which big cats hunt in a group?

3 What are pack hunters?

4 How does a python stop its prey moving?

5 Name two ways spiders stop their prey moving.

6 Which insect predator bites off the head of its prey?

7 How do killer whales find their prey?

8 How many teeth does a great white shark have?

9 How do octopuses confuse their prey?

10 Which predator has the best eyesight?

# Glossary of terms

| | |
|---|---|
| **ambush** | To hide and attack by surprise. |
| **camouflage** | To hide by blending in with surroundings. |
| **fangs** | Long sharp teeth. |
| **harpoon** | To strike with a sharp missile. |
| **pack** | A group of hunting animals, such as wolves or hyenas. |
| **pincers** | Arms or legs used like tongs. |
| **pits** | Holes either side of a snake's head that can detect heat. |
| **predator** | An animal that eats other animals. |
| **prey** | An animal hunted for food. |
| **scavenges** | Feeds on prey that is already dead. |
| **sonic** | To do with sound waves. |
| **stalk** | To follow and try to catch. |
| **talons** | Claws of a bird of prey. |
| **tentacles** | Arm-like or leg-like parts of a sea creature. |
| **venom** | Poison. |
| **venomous** | Poisonous. |

# More resources

## Books

**Polar Bears**
Sandra Markle
Published by First Avenue Editions (ISBN 978-17505460)

**Great White Sharks**
Sandra Markle
Published by Carolrhoda books (ISBN 978-1575057477)

**Deadly Snakes**
Andrew Solway
Published by Heinemann Library (ISBN 978-0431189994)
(also: **Deadly Spiders and Scorpions** (ISBN 978-0431190006)
and **Birds of Prey** (ISBN 978-0431189987)

## Magazines

**BBC wildlife magazine**
Popular monthly wildlife magazine packed with animal features
and pictures.

## Websites

*www.nationalgeographic.com/animals*
Amazing photographs, videos, fact sheets and wallpapers to
download on all kinds of animals including predators.

*www.predatorconservation.com*
The website of the Predator Conservation Trust, with lots of
information on predator animals around the world.

*www.bbc.co.uk/nature/wildfacts/factfiles*
A BBC website with facts, information and photographs on a
searchable database.

## DVDs

**Predators of the Animal World** (1999)
(Cat. no. ASIN B00000JGJR)

**Predators 2: Survival of the Fittest** (2000)
(Cat. no. ASIN  B00004UEEV)

# Answers

1   The spotted hyena

2   Lions

3   Predators that work together to catch prey, like wolves and hyenas

4   It twists around it and strangles it

5   Injecting them with venom or wrapping them in spider silk

6   The praying mantis

7   They send out sonic signals.

8   3000

9   They send out an ink cloud.

10  The eagle

# Index